THE PAGE

DILE

by
Heather Wastie

with illustrations by
Jules ～ cartoonist

LAPAL PUBLICATIONS

Lapal Publications
53 Senneleys Park Road
Birmingham B31 1AE
England
lapalbooks@aol.com
www.lapalbooks.co.uk

First published May 2010

ISBN 978-0-9509238-4-0

Printed in Great Britain by Birches Printers, Walsall
Tel: 01902 605410 www.birchesprinters.co.uk

Contents

FOREWORD

This collection has been brewing for several years. The catalyst for finally getting it into print was the discovery that, having moved house, I was living within walking distance of a cartoonist!

In 1997, when *Until I saw your foot* was published, I spent part of my working life as a recorder teacher, running classes for both children and adults. Since then I have changed direction, but still have fond memories of those classes and the people in them. So before the poetry begins, there are a few snippets from one of those classes.

I would like to thank Lapal Publications for once more giving me the opportunity to publish my work, Glyn Essex for invaluable feedback and Julie Boden for wise words, encouragement and support. A huge thank you also to Jules for working tirelessly to add a new dimension to my poems, not just illustrate them. Finally, thanks to all those people who have inspired the work in this book - most of you know who you are!

Heather Wastie

Memoirs of a recorder tutor

At a schools' workshop I was introducing the various sizes of recorders. I had already played the treble and was holding up a bass recorder to see if anyone knew what it was called. A very keen boy who had had his hand up for every single question (sometimes before I had even asked it) said, "Is it a quadruple?"
Very logical I thought.

The Winterbourne Adult Recorder Class

As a tutor, I had to be careful to maintain a suitable relationship between myself and the students. One longstanding member of the class (the owner of the foot in my previous book, *Until I Saw Your Foot*) wanted to borrow my tenor recorder which I keep in a pair of long brown socks. As I handed it to him someone remarked, "You're not doing his *laundry* now are you?"

It was noted that a female member of the class had sewn flowers onto her jeans. Eventually she admitted that the flowers were there to cover up holes. Someone suggested she sew flowers over the bits of music she couldn't play - surreal!

A new class member compared their first session to being on the M1 for the first time.

First student to teacher: "I'm sorry, I can't hear very well because the battery's gone in my hearing aid."
Second student to class: "Has anyone got any jump leads?"

First student arriving late carrying a fully assembled music stand: "It's such a job on the bus with this!"
Second student: "Yes, and it's difficult now they don't have conductors."

We were discussing the music of John Sheppard. I asked the class how they would describe it. The answer came back, "Woolly".

Smiles and warmth
(as ordered for a lunchtime reading)
or
Bananas from the heart

Here's a smile to keep you warm,
but watch out for me lips -
this red hot colour's not me own
but the sauce from recent chips.

A radiant smile to warm yer chops,
I'll grill you with me teeth
and finish you off with lashings of
me tongue, rare British beef.

A plate of warmth to make you smile,
reheated several times.
I hope it suits yer palate but,
if not, at least it rhymes.

A fruity bowl of curvy smiles,
bananas from the heart,
hand picked in April ninety-eight -
for compost and for art.

Concert etiquette
for Derek

Going to a concert
is a serious affair,
and if you do it wrong
some people love to tut and stare,
so let's go to the concert hall
and try to find out more
from people in the audience
who've done it all before:

There's money in my pocket,
it makes a lovely sound,
so I rattle my coins together
and everyone looks round.
But I can't hear the music -
that woman's gone to sleep.
She's spoiling it by snoring
and this ticket wasn't cheap!

I've got a bag of sweeties
with lovely noisy wrappers,
they're crunchy and they're chewy
and my jaws go like the clappers.
But I can't hear the music -
there's someone eating crisps!
They shouldn't allow such noisy food,
it distracts the soloists.

I like to go to concerts.
I also like to cough
in all the quiet passages,
from Bach to Rachmaninov.
But I can't hear the music -
there's a man in the row behind
whose digital watch is beeping.
Does he think nobody minds?

I always get to concerts
about a minute late.
The stewards refuse to let me in,
it's something that I hate.
For I can't hear the music
from this side of the doors
and when I finally get inside
there's thunderous applause!

I like to clap at concerts,
I clap and clap and clap
whenever anyone walks on stage
and in every available gap.
But I can't hear the music -
I've missed the final chord
in my desperate anxiety
to be the first to applaud.

I find I can't help humming
to tunes I know so well
while my fingertips are drumming
to the theme from *William Tell.*
But I can't hear the music -
there's a man with a mobile phone,
it's playing *The Hall of the Mountain King*
too fast and up a tone.

We try to sit together,
my friend, her friend and me,
to catch up on the latest news -
we whisper, naturally!
But we can't hear the music
and *do not* comprehend
why people have to shuffle out
five minutes before the end.

Going to a concert
is a serious affair,
and if you do it wrong
some people love to tut and stare.
But now you've heard the evidence,
I'm sure you won't forget
the little things that count towards
good concert etiquette.

Bassoonist in love

for June Emerson

I thought of you and missed a vital entry,
I thought of you and played a note too long,
The thought of you has messed up all my breathing
and now it's playing havoc with my tongue.

I thought of you and dotted all my quavers,
I thought of you and played through every rest,
The thought of you has filled up all my minims
and turned them into crotchets, three abreast.

I thought of you and couldn't see my music,
I thought of you and couldn't play in tune,
The thought of you has stripped me of my senses
and left me gazing numbly round the room.

I thought of you and couldn't move my fingers,
I thought of you and couldn't move my brain,
The thought of you has ruined my performance
but now at least there's someone else to blame.

The page-turner's dilemma

Should I enter before the performer,
amble on, look embarrassed, and wait;
or stay off till the artist is comfy?
(When it may look as if I'm just late.)

Will I trip as I step on the platform?
Will I sneeze and demolish a page?
Will I fall and unseat the performer
and be forced to withdraw from the stage?

Is my underarm hygiene important?
Will the hairs up my nose be on view?
Will I drop off to sleep when it's quiet?
Should I read when there's nothing to do?

Should I turn from the top or the bottom?
Should I lift, should I crease, should I curl?
Should I stand at the right or left shoulder?
Should I whip, or peel back and unfurl?

Should I wait till the very last minute
and risk yanking the book off the stand
or adopt a legato slow motion
with a couple of bars still in hand?

Should I sit till engaged in manoeuvres
and then bob up and down like a cork?
Should I stand till the music is over
and be ready to pounce like a hawk?

Should I look for a nod or a gesture?
Will it show when I can't read the score?
Will I flap if my arm starts to tremble?
Will I turn two together, or more?!

There are so many questions to answer -
Where oh where in the world can one learn
this most delicate art, fraught with danger?
It's so hard to know which way to turn.

The harpsichord which, in the second movement of
Handel's A minor Recorder Sonata,
having reached bar 6, recklessly flung off its G# key
(a true story)

Clon-clonk, clonk
clatter clatter clatter clatter clon-clonk, clonk
clatter clatter clatter clatter,
clatter clatter clatter clatter, clatter clatter clatter clatter
clatter clatter clatter clatter, clatter clatter clatter clatter
clatter clatter clatter clatter, clatter clatter clatter clatter
splatter clatter splat!

Where I should have breathed
for Jane

At the beginning
Before the first note
Before I had opened my music
Before I had walked through the door

At the end of the first phrase
After I needed to

In the middle

Where I should have been resting

At the end
When it was all over
When it was not as bad as I thought it would be
At the beginning
Before the first note

Worst side story

Tonight, tonight,
I'll have a rest tonight,
Tonight I'll leave my brain in the car.
Tonight, tonight,
I'll watch the box tonight
and my feet will stay right where they are.

Today has pushed me to the limit,
I hated every minute,
I'm spoiling for a fight.
Stand back, I'll bite
and if you light my fuse I'll ignite
Tonight!

Tonight, tonight
will be a special night,
Tonight I'll talk to no-one at all.
Tonight, tonight,
you won't see me tonight -
don't come round, e-mail, fax, text or call.

Today I don't want any lovin',
there's pizza in the oven
blood red in every bite.
O moon, grow bright,
I'd give a passing vampire a fright
Tonight!

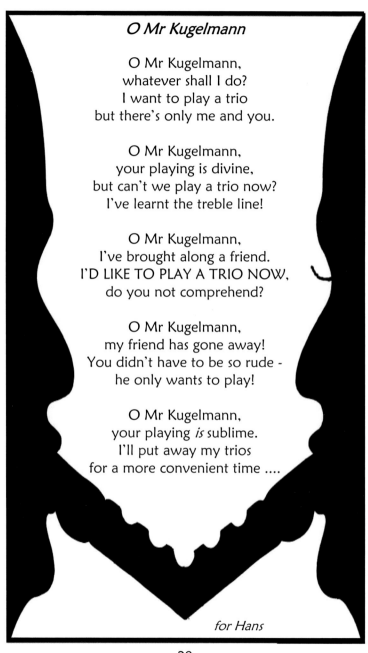

O Mr Kugelmann

O Mr Kugelmann,
whatever shall I do?
I want to play a trio
but there's only me and you.

O Mr Kugelmann,
your playing is divine,
but can't we play a trio now?
I've learnt the treble line!

O Mr Kugelmann,
I've brought along a friend.
I'D LIKE TO PLAY A TRIO NOW,
do you not comprehend?

O Mr Kugelmann,
my friend has gone away!
You didn't have to be so rude -
he only wants to play!

O Mr Kugelmann,
your playing *is* sublime.
I'll put away my trios
for a more convenient time ....

for Hans

What did the big soprano say to the little soprano?
for Mom

My dress is bigger than *your* dress
because *my* lungs are larger than *yours*
and *my* notes are louder than *your* notes,
in fact I sound better outdoors,
while *your* tiny frame merely whimpers,
though you're bursting your veins to be heard;
up here in the second sopranos
you perch like a tiny lost bird.

My breaths are bigger than *your* breaths.
My vibrato could shatter a plate.
My diaphragm's taut as a frisbee,
pinned down by superior weight -
one bounce and a top A goes flying,
one clench and I've made it to B,
but, being a *mezzo* soprano,
I don't often bother with C.

My husband's bigger than *your* husband -
he's joining the basses next week.
He eats small sopranos for breakfast,
especially *thin* ones who *squeak.*
Together we'll drown out the lot of you
and don't think we'll stop at the choir;
we're looking for world domination
as soon as we've sung The Messiah.

In memoriam gigam

Modern Milly, not so thorough,
left her backing tracks at home,
tried to sing the drum and bass, guitar, piano, saxophone
and all the vocals on her own,
sang so loud she very nearly
pulverised the microphone,
danced so hard she almost pushed her
pink stiletto through the floor.
Sorry, Milly, I left early,
beat a passage to the door,
couldn't take a quaver more.

      We bopped to your Boy Lollipop
      and pruned our lips *de-doot-doot-doo*
      but when you launched a brave Titanic,
      left the sinking ship to you.

Now here's the moral: if you ever
leave your backing tracks at home,
heed the tale of Modern Milly,
who abused the microphone.
Don't try *boom boom doo-wop tinkle thwack twang
woah de-doot-doot-doo*
all on your own!

Duet
for Nigel S

What a performance!
You should have been there.
The cut of their cords,
the slick of their hair.

Such vocal projection,
such posture, such style!
Such bold choreography,
bottle and guile.

The louder the music,
the louder they'd shout –
a valiant attempt
to drown it all out.

Their timing was perfect,
the rise and the fall
of their subtle dynamic
astonished us all.

Haiku
for Joe Green

With Dies Irae,
Verdi throws the whole of life
panting at our feet

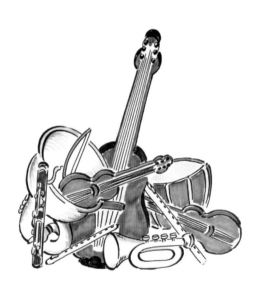

Because I like singing

Is it a kind of blasphemy
for an atheist
to sing a hymn?

If I miss out
all the consonants,
will I get away with it?

Sometimes I'm tempted
to sing *bored*
instead of *Lord*
or *cod*
instead of *God*
like a rebellious child

but I end up looking
like a dull fish,
joining in
with all the best tunes,
trying not to look
as if I mean it.

Playing the piano
for Matthew

When I play the piano,
which I very often do,
I get a funny feeling
and it starts inside my shoe:

First my toes begin to wiggle
and my legs begin to waggle,
then my bottom starts to shuffle
and my shoulders start to ruffle,

then my head begins to joggle
and my arms begin to jiggle
then my fingers start to wobble
like a spider with a giggle!

My fingers start wobbling
because my arms are jiggling
and my arms start jiggling
because my head is joggling

and my head starts joggling
because my shoulders are ruffling
and my shoulders start ruffling
because my bottom is shuffling

and my bottom starts shuffling
because my legs are waggling
and my legs start waggling
because my toes are wiggling,

and every time I play a tune
my toes are full of wiggles
because they're trying very very hard
to reach the pedals!

Tea at Great Grandma's

She liked to flick wet lettuce at my face
and hand out nobs of butter on a knife.
Her tablecloth, pure white and edged with lace
was saved for someone special in her life
who stayed for weekly scrabble after tea
and brought a young accomplice - that was me.
Those musty hours were patient as the clock
which dragged its heavy footsteps round and round,
encircling the contestants, deeply locked
in battle, to exclusion of all sound
save for the anxious sucking of her teeth
as I, in charge of letters, underneath
the table, knowing well what I should do,
made sure that Gran had X, J, K *and* Q.

My plate
for Tom

Scene of many a tortuous battle.
Odds against me from the start.
The adversary -
a battery of broad beans.

Negotiations abandoned.
Under attack from the air.

Enemy circling to reload.
Bring on the bread sauce.
Smother the opposition.

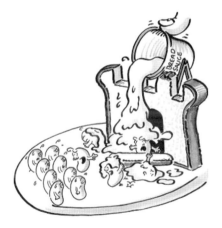

Nothing's really changed.
Still got a lot on my plate.
Still trying to hide my broad beans
under the bread sauce.

The parrot
for Sophie

I once drew a parrot

but it looked like a carrot,
all orange with feathers of green.

So I then drew a carrot

but it looked like a parrot!
(The most beautiful parrot you've seen.)

So I rubbed out the 'p'
and changed it to 'c'
and I rubbed out the 'c'
and changed it to 'p'.

Now my carrot's a parrot
and my parrot's a carrot
and nobody knows except me.

Gina

for Sophie

Gentle Gina, the ballerina.
In your daydreams, have you seen her
dancing on the window-sill?
Day or night, she's never still.

When the spotlight sun shines through,
she'll turn a pirouette for you.

When the sky is painted grey,
her toes will tap your tears away.

And when the dismal darkness falls,
she'll give a hundred curtain calls,

catching roses, blowing kisses,
Gina's magic never misses.

When you're feeling sad or ill,
she'll be there on your window-sill.
Close your eyes and then you'll see her
quietly dancing, gentle Gina.

The lost skipping rope
for Sophie

I'm looking for my skipping rope,
I hope I find it soon.
I'm looking with a telescope
in case it's on the moon.
It might have made a necklace
with all the painted stars
which decorate the darkness
from Earth to planet Mars.

I wish I had my skipping rope,
it's nowhere to be found.
I'm looking with a microscope
in case it's in the ground.
It might be helping earth-worms
to wriggle in and out
or training tiny beetles
to skip and jump about.

I've searched the sky, the earth, the house,
but still I don't succeed.
I've questioned the spaghetti
and followed every lead
and though I'm trying not to mope,
it's really very hard to cope.
So when my birthday comes I hope
I get a *brand new* skipping rope.

Vaughan

Vaughan barked the dog,
he buzzed a bee
and made his sister spill her tea.

Vaughan squawked the budgie,
squeaked a mouse
and chased them wildly round the house.

Vaughan croaked a frog
and yelped the cat.
(He was especially proud of that.)

He roared a lion at the zoo.
I haven't seen him since.
Have you?

GANGLAND
for Matthew

Everybirdy knows that magpies are the bad guys, especially the crows

More than just four

I'm a little bit five
because yesterday
I was only as tall
as my nose

but today I can reach
to the top of my head
without having to stand
on my toes.

Domestic Science

Balancing my bowl on the ample shelf of her bosom,
she picked at my crumble with paint-encrusted claws,
screening it for lumps with a radar sweep of her finger,
more fat in my flour than was tightening round her jaws.

Looking with disdain at my sad attempt at a pudding,
with *my* margarine still embedded in her nails,
casting me aside with a flash of armpit and wrinkles,
she rubbed it well in that a girl like me needs scales.

Whatever you do, don't

Whatever you do, don't look down
or you'll see that your shoes are not brown
as you thought, but an odd shade of red
and they're tied with spaghetti instead
of the laces you've come to expect.
Eyes front, and you'll never suspect.

Whatever you do, don't look down
or you'll see that you're really a clown
and your feeble attempts to move faster
are hampered by freshly made pasta.
Keep looking ahead all day long
and you won't know there's anything wrong.

Late night visitor

Eleven o'clock came and went
without leaving a hint of a scent,
without hanging his coat or his hat,
without dropping a speck on the mat.

Though it's true he committed no sin,
I'd like to know *who* let him in.

Keep off the grass

Don't let the grass grow under your feet -
sprinkle the seeds where there's moisture and heat,
but somewhere that's further away from the street
like under your armpits or inside your nose
and stand on your head for a week while it grows,
so at least it won't clog up the gaps in your toes.

But *don't* let the grass grow under your feet -
you could plant something useful, like barley or wheat
or rapeseed, but don't try a rose.
It's a popular choice for it smells rather sweet
but its flowers are so bright that it's just not discreet
and I hear that the pain never goes.

No, DON'T let the grass grow under your feet
for in time it will just decompose,
then you'll sink through the ground and end up as peat
which leaves terrible stains on your clothes.

Living

Life is a challenge.
   The challenge is living
      Without crying or dying or falling over
         Or losing or failing or moaning or wailing
       Or killing or spilling
      Or hating
      Or keeping somebody waiting
    Annoying, disturbing, upsetting,
  Forgetting your library book,
      Corrupting, erupting, distressing,
        Undressing in mixed company,
          Lying or prying or spying,
            Destroying, mistreating,
              Alarming or harming
               Or sweating
            Or getting people's names wrong,
         Misleading, misreading or bleeding,
        Exceeding the speed limit
     Or drinking and driving
    Or boring or snoring, ignoring
  Or fighting or spitting or swearing
    Or wearing odd socks,
      Being rude to the neighbours,
        Misusing, confusing, abusing, refusing
      Or sneering or jeering or leering or peering,
   Mishearing,
  Mistaking or faking or making a mess,
 Being moody or broody or sulky or grumpy
Or nasty or hasty or sloppy or stroppy or fussy or bossy,
   Malicious, suspicious, officious or vicious
     And yet remaining ambitious.

A peaceful moment

This empty space is
for me, and for once I will
not fill it with words.

Patient
for Vernon

He sits anxiously at her side
smiling hesitantly as I walk in,
then goes back to biting his lip,
eyes flicking back and forth
across her face, shoulders, hair -

long, blonde, *in lovely condition to say it's bleached,*
and you can see how much it's grown since last time.
She tells the stylist how good the gel is
that she gets from an Indian bloke on the market
but if you blast it with the diffuser it gets bitty
and anyway her hair doesn't curl like it used to.

All three of them discuss the perils of dying.
He says he died his hair black once
and it ran down his face
and he couldn't get it off
and he'd gone to pick his son up from school
and people in cars kept papping at him.
She laughs, clutching the belly of her gown.

For two and a half hours he sits beside her, expectant,
fascinated by every part of the procedure.
You'd think from his look,
from his supportive, understanding presence,
his immersed involvement in her condition,
that she was about to give him
a new heir,
not new hair.

Washing day

The fat clouds roll up,
rubbing their hands with glee,
waiting for the floor show.

Noisy neighbours

Feet up.
Eyes closed.
Not a sound.

* * * * * * * * * * * * * * * * * *

Through the wall,
a familiar forty-something voice
rises to its ceiling:

"Terry!"
"TERRY!"
"T E A R R A A A A Y!!"

"TURN IT DOWN!!"

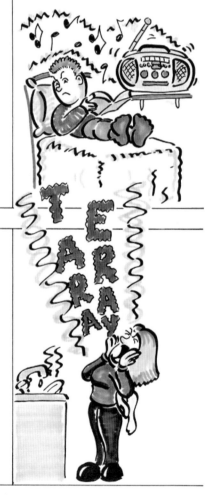

View from the kitchen window
for Jack

Across the road
there stands
a bronzed statue,
a man of iron
wrought from his gate.

He leans without a shirt,
preserving a hard-earned tan,
his full muscles learning patience -
content now to simply lift an arm
or shift his head
in time with the rhythm of the road.

His eyes alive
with passing smiles,
his ears fine-tuned
to the croon of a horn,
his fingertip sparking the pavement,
he tirelessly handles
a hundred visitors a day.

37 Holly Bush Street

37 Holly Bush Street,
a few doors up from the Mission,
lying in bed on a Sunday morning
trying hard not to listen
to the slowest singing in Cradley Heath,
a rousing hymnotic dirge:
"May all God's notes be joined as one,
Slide heavenward and converge!
And when we've emptied out our lungs
And, Lord, can sing no more,
We'll quench our lasting thirst for thee
In the *'olly Bush* next door."

37 Holly Bush Street,
a few doors down from Dingley's,
source of kali and sherbet dabs
and chocolate drops sold singly.
And there goes Alice in carpet slippers,
fulfilling her daily pledge,
striding uphill to a soul in need
with a plate full of meat and two veg.
And late in the darkness goes 'Uncle' George
who brought in the coal at New Year.
As he rolls down the road with his darling Gladys,
piercing the closing-time air
comes "Good night, Gladys!" and "Goodnight, George!"
all down the street and beyond,
echoing through the silent years
till front doors bang shut and are gone.

37 Holly Bush Street,
the heart of a microcosm,
from the boy who dribbled and never grew old
to the woman who flaunted her bosom.
And one day they shovelled us into a heap
and threw all the pavements away,
stopping just short of the pub and the Mission,
but leaving me nowhere to play.

Enough's enough

It's all the maintenance I hate,
removing grease and adding paint,
sanding down and shaving off.
At forty-three, I've had enough.
I'm sick of clipping, tired of mowing;
it's time my nails and hair stopped growing.

Life
would be torture
without talcum

Days
would be crappy
without cream

Mornings
would languish
without lotion

If I didn't
have deodorant
I'd scream

Aerobics

A room full of knees
in matching pairs

smooth mountain ranges
devoid of hairs

deforestation
on human scale

the prostrate view of a
flushed female

Personal space

Perfume should be timed
so that it orbits the wearer
at a distance of no more than
five centimetres.

It gets right up my
nose when the equivalent of
Saturn's rings hits my carefully
balanced atmosphere.

Hair wars

They poke from our noses
and spring from our faces;
they float unattended
to all sorts of places.

They sprout on our kneecaps,
our ankles and shins;
in clusters they stick
to the bottoms of bins.

They drip from our heads
and inhabit the shower,
embedded in soap,
trying patience for hours.

They clog up the plughole,
turn grey when you're older,
desert all their friends,
show up on your shoulder.

They fall into soup,
reproduce without mating
and tickle your lip
while your lover is waiting.

You can't flick them off
when they stick to your finger,
they cling to your cloth,
and the curly ones linger

on tiles, in the bath,
on the rim of the loo.
You wipe one away and hey
presto, there's two.

They may not be your hairs
or her hairs or his,
you cannot avoid them,
that's just how it is.

PSD

The doctor says I've got
"Public Speakers' Disease"

Apparently there's "concern"
over a possible "epidemic"

The only "symptom"
is an itchy "rash"
either side of the head

and the only "cure"
is to stop scratching

Woman in a Ford
dedicated to ungrateful drivers

I am a fish
and this is my tank.
I climbed in this morning
and immediately sank.

You may think I'm chewing
by the drift of my chin,
but that's just a fish
breathing out and then in.

You may think I'm gawping
as I watch you sail past,
but I can't help my face -
it's the way I've been cast.

For I am a fish
and fishes don't smile
and they haven't got hands
to wave thanks. Life is vile.

Late encounter

I'd rather too young than too old.
I'd rather too hot than too cold.
I'd rather not tell you my age
In case you cool off at this stage.

Conversation stopper
for Laurie, who donated the first line

If you mention the pension
as you munch on your luncheon,
eat each portion with caution,
or I'll venture your denture
will have wrecked your conjecture.

A prayer for preservation

O my life, preserve me

from bad perfume and floral frock,
from underskirt and deafening clock,

from dangling specs and lilac hair,
from bunions, pearls and tupperware,

from see-through hat and plastic mac,
from talk of stroke or heart attack,

from nights that toss and days that pass,
from dentures grinning in a glass,

o my life, preserve me.

Notice to visitors
for David, commissioned by Sophie & Matthew

Please do not adjust
the dust
in this building.

Each particle
has been restored,
reclaimed from the original,
replaced exactly where it would have been
on August 27th 1880.

Visitors are requested
not to cough
splutter
sneeze
or in any way create
gusts.

Sniffing is prohibited.
At the end of the tour
all noses will be thoroughly searched
and fingertips examined for traces
of dust
belonging to
the Trust.

Thank you.

The proposal
for Geoff

You cornered me by the cooker,
sizzling.

You played Widor's Toccata on the cutlery,
spoons timed to perfection.

I swooned
with the heat of your curry
and we danced
in the silvery gaslight.

Then I clocked your Rioja
and decided that my kitchen
was definitely big enough
for both of us.

Making friends with Sid
for Clare

Sid the punk zimmer is gothic in black,
his leather pyjamas have studs up the back,

his mohican haircut stands proudly erect,
adorning his cross bar, commanding respect.

Sid the punk zimmer is tattooed with chains
which clatter around him and charge up his veins.

His ankles are pierced (how the walking stick grins!
for dangling politely are six nappy pins).

Sid the punk zimmer has practised his stance,
his feet wide apart and his hips for her hands:

To show that she loves him she's painted his smile
in soft pink nail polish. He's hers, for a while.

And when she returns him I'll bet you ten quid
that no other patient will christen him Sid.

A Lancashire lass brought down to earth
a (partly) true story

I was out with my friend Freda in her Fiat 126,
its roof wide open on a sunny day,
when all at once before us walking softly down the street
was Jesus, just a hundred yards away.

I should tell you that this Jesus wasn't biblical or ought
but just a chap who liked to dress the same
and got himself arrested when the Bingo queue complained
he'd hassled them for being on the game.

Well, we hadn't spotted Jesus down our way for quite a while
so naturally we both were quite transfixed,
and Freda didn't notice that the traffic lights had changed
to red, and she was clocking 36!

I should point out that our Freda is a tiny little lass,
while me, I'm six foot four without me boots
and haven't got much headroom in a Fiat 126,
so when she jams her brakes on, up I shoots!

I ascended through the sunroof in a cloud of purple smoke
and, looking down on Jesus from above,
I met his icy glare as he began to shake his head,
"In future, wear your flamin' seatbelt, love."

The lonely pot-hole

There was a young pot-hole called Pete
who confessed to a life incomplete.
He applied for assistance
to enrich his existence,
so the council resurfaced his street.

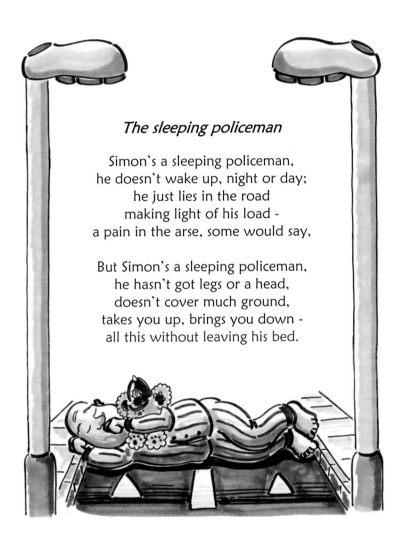

The sleeping policeman

Simon's a sleeping policeman,
he doesn't wake up, night or day;
he just lies in the road
making light of his load -
a pain in the arse, some would say,

But Simon's a sleeping policeman,
he hasn't got legs or a head,
doesn't cover much ground,
takes you up, brings you down -
all this without leaving his bed.

The lady from Kidderminster

A lady from Kidderminster
was worried that time was aginster.
What really convinster,
this lovely old spinster,
was when the hairdresser bluerinster.

Royal intent

An ambitious old man from Barnt Green
thought his daughter should one day be queen,
so he sent her cv
to the next king-to-be
every year, from the age of eighteen.

The testament of Bill

There was an old builder called Noah
who heard there would soon be a shower,
so he built a big boat
so his assets would float
but it sank after just half an hour.

There was a young builder called Bill
whose boat had been built with more skill.
It came down with a thud
at the end of the flood
on the top of a whopping great hill

There was a reporter called Sid
who saw what young William did.
But he got on the blower
and said it was Noah,
for he'd tell any fib for a quid.

The cycling widow
for Ted

I here relate a tale of woe,
Of one in deep despair -
A maid who took her chances with
A breed of man most rare.

At first he seemed a normal chap
Until, O fateful deed,
He bought himself a bicycle,
Not knowing where 'twould lead.

For that was just the start of it -
Before she could protest,
He'd gone and bought another one.
He said 'twas for the best.

He wooed her with his touring frame
Until she said, "I do",
And then she had to face the truth -
He couldn't make do with two.

One day he broke the news to her:
"A racer I will be!"
And then revealed his Battaglin,
Which meant he now had three.

She begged of him to stem the tide,
But still he wanted more.
"I think I'll have a blue one next."
She hoped he'd stop at four.

"All top men have an alloy frame -
I've ordered mine today."
She carefully avoided what
She'd half a mind to say,

For surely now he had the lot
And five would be enough.
But little did she know that he
Was into rougher stuff.

A track-bike came as number six.
He said it was the last.
But, sad to say, it was too late,
For she was sinking fast.

When last I saw this hapless maid,
She staggered all forlorn
From what was once her kitchen,
Wits and patience tried and torn.

Her vain attempts to scale the heap
Of saddles, spokes and chains
Were just too much for her to take
And little now remains

Of what was once a carefree lass
Who made this one mistake -
She wed a man who bought a bike
And couldn't find the brake.

Enjoying the view

Oh how I love to see your back,
I love to see the back of you -
Of all the views that I could choose,
I couldn't choose a better view:

Your pockets bulging inner-tubes
and levers, inches from my teeth;
your torso dancing to the beat
of thighs in tandem underneath.

Your shoulders my horizon and
your head eclipsing what's to come,
you toss a knowing smile behind
as lovingly I stroke your bum.

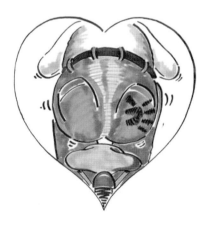

L'Etape du Tour 1996 – a haiku reflection

(L'Etape is a stage of the Tour de France ridden by amateurs under Tour conditions)

Six thousand cyclists
and the light doesn't work
in the portaloo.

Bravo! Courage! Who
Allez, allez! am I
Vives les femmes! to you?

Hard enough ascent
without flies drinking my sweat,
perched on my nose.

A lone gone rider
rambling and rolling
half way up a col.

Can't give up now.
Flies fight for my yoghurt bar.
Tyres bite the road.

Tour de France fake
pops one more dried apricot.
Bon repas! she hears.

A bone-dry baguette,
after ten saddle-sore hours –
what a frame up!

Photo finish –
teetering helmet,
toppling smile.

The road to success

In the bookshop window
enticingly sits
my first collection

attractively placed
alongside the fabulous new edition
of the Birmingham A to Z.

In memory of John Greaves Smith
who illustrated *UNTIL I SAW YOUR FOOT*
and drew this cartoon

The art of poetry

Here sits John, he labours on,
a shapely figure by his side,
sweating over half-drawn sheets
until he's fully satisfied
that all his drawings fill the space
that's not already occupied
by words. And could you only see
his face, you'd find he's quite cross-eyed.

Please remain seated for the British Anthem

God save our gravy boat,
keep our roast beef afloat,
God save our greens.
Send apple pie to us
when we are ravenous,
pour custard over us.
God save baked beans.

Nonstruments

by Heather Wastie & Geoff Cox

Trombola   an instrument played by turning a handle and choosing a note at random

Octoboe   an oboe for 8 players

Frugalhorn   a horn which has no unnecessary notes

Cleverchord   a keyboard instrument with more notes than it knows what to do with

Pianofifty   new, improved piano – 25% better

Trambone   obsolete instrument powered by overhead cables

Silophone   huge smelly instrument often played by farm workers

Piano accordial   friendly keyboard in a choice of fruity flavours

Percushion   instrument designed for easy listening